FREE
INDEED

*Living Life in Light
of the Biblical
View of Freedom*

FREE INDEED

Living Life in Light of the
Biblical View of Freedom

ART LINDSLEY

INSTITUTE FOR
FAITH, WORK
& ECONOMICS

First Edition, 2016
ISBN 978-0-9975369-2-8

Published by the
Institute for Faith, Work & Economics
8400 Westpark Drive
Suite 100
McLean, Virginia 22102

www.tifwe.org

CONTENTS

INTRODUCTION 1

CHAPTER 1: THE BIBLICAL VIEW OF FREEDOM—
A BIRD'S EYE VIEW 4

"Freedom from" or "Freedom to"? 4

Freedom in Greek Philosophy 5

Freedom in the Old Testament 6

Freedom in the New Testament 8

CHAPTER 2: FREEDOM APPLIED—SEVEN PREMISES 15

Premise 1: Political, economic and religious
freedom are dependent on each other 15

Premise 2: Biblical freedom is based on a moral foundation .. 18

Premise 3: Biblical freedom upholds private property 22

Premise 4: Biblical freedom limits government power 24

Premise 5: Biblical freedom and innovation 33

Premise 6: Biblical freedom always considers the Fall 36

Premise 7: Biblical freedom
encourages toward true progress 37

CONCLUSION 43

ABOUT THE AUTHOR 45

ABOUT THE INSTITUTE FOR
FAITH, WORK & ECONOMICS 48

INTRODUCTION

Freedom is the last thing that should be taken for granted. Because of the Fall, we are in bondage to sin. True freedom necessitates the Spirit's work to change our heart and redirect our lives, which will otherwise give way to entropy. Left to ourselves things tend toward disorder, a loss of spiritual life, a decline in vitality. However, Christ's redemption of our lives allows us to be more and more what we are created to be. If we continue in his words we will know the truth, and the truth will make us free (John 8:32). If Jesus makes you free, "you will be free indeed" (John 8:36).

The Bible's vision of an ideal state of living includes more than this inner freedom. Christ has set us free, and we need to live accordingly because God is working out good things through us – including the freedom and flourishing of others. Our inner freedom should lead us to outer freedom. For this reason, political, economic, and religious freedom should not be taken for granted, either. God's people were slaves in Egypt for 400 years. God heard their prayers and raised up Moses to go to Pharaoh and say, "Let my people go." God demonstrated his power time and again. First, there were ten plagues. Then he parted the Red Sea just as the situation seemed hopeless, with his people stuck between Migdol and the sea with the Egyptian armies bearing down on them. When they arrived on the other side, they celebrated. Miriam and the other women danced and threw dust in the air. They were free. Yet they still had to face time in the wilderness, times of rebellion from God's ways, the giving of the Law and conquering the Promised Land. Freedom from outer bondage at the Exodus led to the quest for inner freedom. It is not enough to have one without the other.

The same is true today. In America particularly, freedom should not be taken for granted. We fought for our freedom, and it has been an American cornerstone ever since the Revolution. The Declaration of Independence notes that certain "inalienable rights" include "life, liberty and the pursuit of happiness." Patrick Henry famously said, "Give me liberty or give me death."

The First Amendment states, "Congress shall make no law respecting an establishment of religion, or prohibiting the free exercise thereof." Freedom of speech, the freedom of the press, and the freedom of assembly are all guaranteed. These freedoms are still upheld, but without vigilance there is always the prospect of lawmakers, executive orders, and the courts taking away some of those freedoms we have assumed will always be there.

Outer, political threats are not the only ones with the potential to erode our freedom. There are also philosophical and moral threats as well. As relativism increasingly encroaches on our society, the notion of objective truth has been discarded by many. Reality is what you want it to be. Instead of conforming their desires to the truth, many would rather conform "truth" to their desires. With nothing any longer inalienable (or objective), what will become of life and liberty?

We, as believers, need to go back to the source—the Bible—and look anew at the biblical view of freedom. This study explores the biblical view of freedom in the Old and New Testament (Chapter 1). It also looks at whether political, economic, and religious freedom are grounded in the Bible (Chapter 2). Although many seek freedom of some sort, the biblical view of freedom is distinctive. The Bible points toward inner and outer freedom as an ideal state. Although God has ordained government, the Bible limits its function and repeatedly warns about government taking ever more of our life and freedoms. When human power becomes too concentrated, there is always the real danger that sin will corrupt and lead to disastrous results.

If we believe in the Bible, we should promote its principles. That belief will lead us to desire inner and outer freedom for ourselves and others. It will also lead us toward political, economic, and religious freedom. We need to ponder these truths in the perilous times in which we live. If we don't consider and act on these truths, we may find our freedoms and those of our children increasingly eroded. We may soon be at a point where we need to stand up or lose our freedom.

If we believe that biblical values can lead to a flourishing society, we need to promote these truths and vote for people that advocate similar values. That means being informed, speaking up when necessary, voting our conscience, and continuing to advocate for freedom in political, economic, and religious spheres.

All these things begin with understanding the biblical view of freedom and living life in light of the amazing truth that in Christ; we are free indeed.

CHAPTER 1
THE BIBLICAL VIEW OF FREEDOM—A BIRD'S EYE VIEW

"Freedom from" or "Freedom to"?

If we are going to have a free and flourishing society, it would be valuable to ponder the biblical perspective on freedom in the Old and New Testament. This chapter will not examine it in the depth it deserves, but it will give a bird's eye view with a quick survey of the subjects. Just about everybody wants freedom, but there are many different views as to what it entails. Biblical freedom, in contrast to other views, does not mean doing whatever you feel like doing. Freedom paradoxically involves throwing off the bondage of sin and becoming a servant of Christ. When we throw off the lies and deceptions to which we are so often captive, we will know the truth, and the truth will set us free.

Throughout human history, people of all cultures have sought freedom. Some have emphasized inner spiritual or emotional freedom, and others freedom from external restraints (such as slavery or political freedom). Hindus seek an experience of oneness with the universe that frees them from the illusion of this world of distinction. Buddhists seek enlightenment that involves a detachment from desiring anything in this world. Atheists want to be free from the constraints of any objective moral rules.

In the political arena, there are a variety of liberation theologies. Gustavo Gutiérrez wrote his *Theology of Liberation* with a focus on the political and economic situation in Latin America. James Cone wrote *A Black Theology of Liberation* to develop a black theology that identified with the oppressed. Others have developed feminist liberation theology that focuses on cultural problems that have limited women's freedom. Most of the above perspectives involve a freedom from constraints but are not clear about what the liberated situation would look like. This "freedom from" constraints perspective is at the heart of our secular culture. In this chapter, we will discuss the biblical view of freedom, first contrasting it with other views so we can see its significance more clearly.

Many people in our culture believe freedom to be a lack of norms, rules, or laws restraining us from doing what we want to do or be. You often hear the refrain "whatever is true for you is true for you, and whatever is true for me is true for me. Nobody can tell me what to do." People who hold to this view believe in "freedom from" any external values. This freedom is limited if God exists. In his film *Crimes and Misdemeanors*, Woody Allen portrays God as a cosmic eye who is always watching us. You can't escape his gaze and his judgment of your life. Jean Paul Sartre, the atheist existentialist, went so far as to argue that if God exists, we couldn't be free. God would be like a cosmic voyeur, always looking through the keyhole watching every little thing in our lives. This kind of "freedom from" something is not the biblical view of freedom, which is more of a "freedom from in order to be free to." We need to be freed from bondage to sin in order to be free to serve Jesus. It is only in the latter state that we can know the freedom and flourishing that we were created to experience.

Freedom in Greek Philosophy

There are different perspectives on freedom throughout history. The Greek view is perhaps the most directly influential in our culture. Before we look more directly at the biblical view of freedom, it would be helpful to draw a further contrast with the classical Greek view of freedom. In Greek philosophy, freedom, *eleutheros*, was primarily used in a political sense. First, someone who is free is a full citizen of the city state, *polis*, in contrast to a slave who did not have the rights of a citizen. To be free meant to have freedom to speak openly and decide what you want to do. It is important to note that this freedom was fenced in by the law. In order to preserve freedom, there needed to be political order governed by law that was enforced. Note that:

> Freedom, for Plato and Aristotle, is essential to a state. The best constitution guarantees the greatest freedom (Thucydides). This freedom is freedom within the law which establishes and secures it.... Law protects freedom against the caprice of the tyrant or the mass.... Democracy achieves this best by allowing the same rights to all citizens (cf. Plato, Aristotle, Herodotus). [However, if] the law of self replaces the law of the politeía....it leads to the rise of demagogues and opens the door to tyranny.[1]

In other words, this freedom was within the structure of the law.

In Stoic philosophy, freedom was inwardly directed. Since people could not always control internal events, emphasis was placed on an internal detachment from this world and anything that would bind you to it, such as anger, anxiety, pity, and the fear of death. Individual reason was to be brought into harmony with the cosmic reason. There was a constant struggle to maintain this detachment (*atarchia*). Freedom was inner freedom for the Stoics and primarily outer freedom for Plato and Aristotle.

Freedom in the Old Testament

In the Old Testament, freedom was primarily a freedom from slavery. There was provision in the Law for the freedom of Israelite slaves (probably like indentured servants) every seven years in the sabbatical year (Exod. 21:2ff). The previous "owner" was to be generous in giving gifts that would enable these freed ones to set up a new life (Deut. 15:12ff).

In a larger sense, freedom was precarious for Israelites. God by his grace delivered them from slavery in Egypt (Exod. 20:2; Deut. 7:8). They repeatedly needed to be delivered from foreign oppression by the Judges. Time and again, a generation came along that didn't know and follow the Lord, and a foreign conqueror would make their lives difficult until the Lord raised up a deliverer. When God's people were disobedient, they often lost their freedom. The Assyrian conquest of the kingdom (II Kings 17:7-23) and the Babylonian captivity of the southern kingdom (II Kings 21:10-15; 22:19f; 23:25ff) are illustrations of this pattern. In later Judaism, freedom movements arose to gain political freedom in order to allow religious freedom (among other things). The Maccabeans and the Zealots are only a couple illustrations of such movements.

This freedom was often referenced in the prophets. Jesus's inaugural sermon echoed this theme (Luke 4:18-19). Isaiah 61:1 says:

> The Spirit of the Lord God is upon me,
> Because the Lord has anointed me
> To bring good news to the afflicted;
> He has sent me to bind up the brokenhearted,
> To proclaim liberty to the captives,
> and freedom to the prisoners.

This proclamation of "liberty" and "freedom" was a mark of the Messiah's message.

There is a consistent thread through the Old Testament pointing to the need for inner and spiritual renewal. Many passages could be cited, but a couple in particular illustrate this theme. In Ezekiel 36:26-30 it says,

> Moreover, I will give you a heart of flesh. And I will put my Spirit within you and cause you to walk in my statutes, and you will be careful to observe my ordinances and you will live in the land that I gave your forefathers...and I will call for the grain and multiply it, and I will not bring famine on you. And I will multiply the fruit of the tree and the produce of the field.

Notice here that the inner rebirth leads to outer flourishing and safety.

Similarly, the classic passage in II Chronicles 7:14 says, "If...my people who are called by my name humble themselves and pray and seek my face and turn from their wicked ways, then I will hear from heaven, will forgive their sin, and will heal their land." Again, the inner change leads to outer or external consequences that extend not only to forgiveness but to healing in the land. Both inner and outer freedom are valued.

Freedom in the New Testament

The predominant note of the New Testament is not political freedom but freedom in Christ from bondage to sin, the Law, Satan, the old man, and death. It is not that political freedom or freedom from slavery was unimportant but that there was an even deeper bondage that had to be overcome first. With the Greeks, the problem was with the mind. In the New Testament, the problem was the bondage of the will. Even if you were politically free, you could still be in bondage.

This is still true today. Human will is not at this present time neutral but is captivated by sin. Humans by nature "love the darkness" and "hate the light" (John 3:19:20). Jesus speaks about this freedom in the classic verses in John 8:31-32: "Jesus therefore was saying to those Jews who had believed in Him, 'If you abide in my words, then you are truly disciples of mine, and you shall know the truth, and the truth shall make you free.'"

The scribes and Pharisees immediately respond to this statement of Jesus by arguing that they are Abraham's offspring and have never been slaves, so how can Jesus say that "You shall become free?" Jesus responds that anyone who sins becomes a slave of sin, but "if therefore the Son shall make you free, you shall be free indeed" (John 8:36). Graciously applied to our lives, Jesus's death and resurrection liberates us from bondage to sin so that we can live a redirected life. Calvin points out that although we have freedom, it may not be perfect. "Freedom has its degrees according to the measure of their faith; and therefore Paul, though clearly made free, still groans and longs after perfect freedom (Rom. 7:24)."[2]

It is the truth that will make us free. We are, in our natural sinful state, captive to lies. We don't see reality as it is. We deny what we know deep down is true (Rom. 1:20-25), "exchanging the truth of God for a lie" (Rom. 1:25). We live in a state of unreality. If truth is that which corresponds to reality, then throwing off lies and deception frees us to see reality for what it is. We see our own slavery to sin and can receive forgiveness and new power to live in accordance with reality. We can be what we were created to be. Truth leads to freedom.

We are historical beings that have a past, present, and future. We don't reinvent ourselves at each moment but are influenced by past patterns and choices. We are according to the old self (sinful nature) directed away from God, saying, in effect, "My will be done." In Christ, we are freed from this bondage in order to say "Thy will be done." We were headed down a road away from God and have been turned around 180 degrees by God's grace so that we are now pursuing our Lord rather than running away from him. We were serving sin, but now we are serving Christ.

But how can service or being a servant be freedom? Because we are made in a particular way, for a purpose, and to function in a designated fashion. One analogy sometimes used is a train. If a train stays on the tracks, it can function well in transporting people and goods from one place to another. If the train goes off the tracks, it leads to pain (and death) for people and a destruction of its cargo. The train needs the tracks to function as it is designed to do. There are limits to where that train can go and the path it needs to follow.

To use another analogy, consider a car. All cars come with manufacturers' recommendations for maximum efficiency. You need to change the oil or the spark plugs at regular intervals. For most cars, you don't put diesel fuel in the gas tank because it causes real problems. Similarly, you don't put water or sugar in the gas tank or it will make the car run poorly or stop it altogether. Just as with the train and the car, there are certain laws, rules, and norms that need to be followed in order to flourish as a human being. We need to follow the Creator's instructions for recommended use as given in the Bible. God's laws or Jesus's commands are not arbitrary but show us the way to joy. This way to joy must involve saying "no" to certain actions or patterns of life that will get us off track. God's character, his revelation in the Bible, and our own nature correspond to each other. We are to be holy because God is holy (I Pet. 1:16). To act in an unholy fashion is to violate God our Creator, his word, and our own being. There are direct consequences to us for violating God's specifications for how to live. We need an intimate relationship with God, closeness to other people, clear vocational direction, proper sexual conduct, sleep, exercise, and nutrition. If we habitually fall short in any of these areas it can lead to dissatisfaction, lack of purpose, a feeling of inadequacy, or even a crisis of meaning or purpose in our life.

There is a structure to reality rooted in God's nature, his creation, and our own being. We can choose to live autonomously, attempting to be "free from" any restriction, but we will never experience true freedom by following that path. True freedom is living the way we were created to live. Another way of describing this life after the Fall is that we serve Christ our Redeemer. We are created in, through, by, and for him (Col. 1: 16). This service, not surprisingly, leads to flourishing. This truth will make us free (John 8:32). In Christ we are free indeed (John 8:36).

The Apostle Paul expounds on the implications of this freedom more fully. See especially Romans 6:18f where we are said to be "freed from sin" so that we can be "slaves to righteousness" (Rom. 6:18). Later, he writes that we are "freed from sin" to be "enslaved to God" (Rom. 6:22). Being "enslaved to God" leads to "eternal life" (vs. 22 and 23) and a fullness of life in the present time.

We are not only freed from sin but also freed from death. Paul says that the outcome of our sin is death (Rom. 6:21) and that the "wages of sin is death" (Rom. 6:23). But Christ has now freed us from the power of death. Note, "Death is swallowed up in victory. O death, where is your sting? ...but thanks be to God, who gives us the victory through our Lord Jesus Christ" (I Cor. 15:54-57). We may fear dying, but we need not fear death itself.

We are also freed from the Law (Rom. 7:3-6). It is not that the Law is bad. In fact, it is said to be "holy and righteous and good" (Rom. 7:12). The Law is even said to be "spiritual" (Rom. 7:14). What, then, are we "freed from"? We are freed from trying to earn our salvation, from duty as a wearisome practice, from the condemnation in our own nature, from having disobeyed the Law. We are not "under the Law but under grace" in that sense (Romans 6:14). But it is not a contradiction of this when Jesus says, "If you love me, you will obey my commandments." We are now freed from the condemnation and external adherence to the Law in order to now serve out of hearts full of grace, out of desire (not merely duty), and joyous obedience.

We are now called to freedom. Paul writes in Galatians, "It was for freedom that Christ set us free" (Gal. 5:1) and "You were called to freedom" (Gal. 5:13). We now experience the glorious liberty of being children of God (Rom. 8:21). We have the Spirit and "where the Spirit of the Lord is there is liberty" (II Cor. 3:17).

We are free but nevertheless subject to the "law of liberty" (James 1:25, and again in James 2:12). Peter Davids says of James's phrase, "He feels perfectly comfortable with enjoying grace within the structure of ethical rules."[3] Similarly, Alec Motyer maintains, "When we come into bondage to the Word of God we come into freedom, because the Word liberates us from the lustful pull of our own nature, and brings us on via the pathway of hard obedience, into new realms of living for God. It is the Law of Liberty."[4] Law and liberty are not contradictory. Just as a train needs tracks in order to experience "trainness," and a car needs manufacturers' specifications to continue in its "carness," so humans need to follow the Creator's manual of guidelines to experience "humanness."

The emphasis of the New Testament is not political, economic, or religious freedom. However, there is a sense in which we can say, as we saw in the Old

Testament, that new inner freedom eventually leads to consequences in the outer world.

Jesus did not fight, as some expected the Messiah to do, for a violent revolutionary overthrow of the Romans. But there are passages that point towards the importance of personal and political freedom. In I Corinthians 7, Paul emphasizes that the believer should stay in the condition in which they were called (I Cor. 7:20, 24). However, if the slave had an opportunity to be free, he or she should take it. "Were you called while a slave? Do not worry about it; but if you are able also to become free, rather do that" (I Cor. 7:21). In Paul's letter to Philemon, the Apostle asks him to receive back Onesimus, "no longer a slave but more than a slave, a beloved brother" (Philem.16). He is urged to "accept him as you would me" (Philem. 17). Paul believes that Philemon will "do even more than what I say." Presumably, this is an urging for Philemon to declare Onesimus the slave free.

The inner freedom Christ came to bring has often been the garden out of which other freedoms grow. The themes of Exodus, "Let my people go," and of Jesus's sermon at his home synagogue in Luke 4 – freedom to the captive – have often been preached. Like Jesus we "proclaim justice" (Matt. 12:18-21) with mercy and compassion. The Holy Spirit is sent to convict concerning sin, righteousness, and judgment (John 16:7f). It seems that this applies not only in personal life but in public life as well. We are to be prophetic – proclaiming his excellencies in a world of darkness (I Pet. 2:9-10). While we can have inner freedom without outer freedom, it is better to have both. The inner freedom gives birth to freedom in public life.

Redemption, above all, applies to all of life. Not only are we redeemed from our sin (personal), we are brought into a new community – the Body of Christ (I Cor. 12:13) (corporate). Our redemption, though, extends beyond the personal and corporate to the whole cosmos. Acts 3:21 says that God's ultimate goal is the "restoration of all things." The whole "creation itself will also be set free from its slavery to corruption into the freedom of the glory of the children of God" (Rom. 8:21). We will ultimately live on a new earth. There are two

Greek words for new – *neos*, meaning totally new, and *kainos*, meaning renewed. Almost every time the Bible uses the word new, *kainos* (renewed) is used. God's redemption will extend to all of life.

Freedom cannot be limited to inner transformation but must of necessity extend to all of life. Jesus not only preached and taught, but healed people's bodies. People were freed inwardly and outwardly. It should not be surprising that where Christ's inner freedom is experienced, the natural outworking is towards political, economic, and religious freedom. There are many biblical passages and themes that demonstrate the holistic freedom and redemption that Jesus came to inaugurate.

No wonder that believers have been on the forefront of freedom movements for the abolition of slavery both past (i.e. William Wilberforce) and present (i.e. International Justice Mission). Many believers have worked to fight for religious freedom nationally and internationally (i.e. Barnabas Fund). We are called to fight against injustice wherever we see it in personal and public life.

Freedom from the bondage to sin, the Law, death, and lies about reality will inevitably push further and further out till it leads to freedom in all areas of life. Inner freedom often has led to outer freedom.

Here are some implications from what we have observed.

1. Freedom is not autonomy or doing what you feel like doing without any constraints.

2. Freedom involves structure. Bondage to Christ allows us to be free to be what we are created to be.

3. Freedom is within the context of Law. We are not under obedience to the Law as a condition of salvation, but the moral Law and Christ's commands give us a guide to know how to live and love.

4. We are truly free when we know the truth about ourselves and the world. This means throwing off the lies and deceptions to which we are so often captive.

5. Salvation is not primarily political liberation (as in some theologies). But God often intervened when his people were oppressed by unjust totalitarian leaders (Exodus, Judges).

6. Inner renewal often leads to outer consequences and renewal of the land.

7. The Bible doesn't prescribe one type of government, but freedom (political, economic, and religious) is consistent with, not contradictory to, the Bible.

8. Inner freedom inevitably drives toward outer freedom. You can have political (economic and religious) freedom and still be in bondage to sin. You can have inner freedom in an oppressed situation. But inner and outer freedoms are the most ideal state for human beings (Micah 4:4).

With this background in mind, it is not surprising that freedom has become a cry for many believers. Believers should be the freest to enjoy life and God's creation, as long as it is within the structure of how God has made us. We are not free from God-ordained obligations, but we are free to live life as God intended it to be lived.

CHAPTER 2
FREEDOM APPLIED—SEVEN PREMISES

The Bible upholds an ideal state of inner and outer freedom. Biblical freedom is defined by the structure of morality in Scripture (biblical laws and commandments). Are political, economic, and religious freedom consistent with biblical values? How can we apply this view of freedom to various aspects of society? Here are seven premises that apply the biblical view of freedom to various aspects of life and demonstrate further aspects of a free society from a biblical perspective.

Premise 1: Political, economic and religious freedom are dependent on each other.

George Washington repeatedly referenced (about fifty times) a verse from the Bible that expressed his vision for America.[5] It is Micah 4:4, which talks about a future where each person, "Will sit under his vine and under his fig tree, with no one to make them afraid."

Note that they will enjoy the fruits of their labors – "sit." They will enjoy their private property – "his" vine and "his" fig tree. They will be in a protected and secure environment with "no one to make them afraid."

This requires freedom from undue intrusion in our lives, private ownership, and freedom from fear. Preventing this intrusion requires emphasizing three principles: freedom, fulfillment, and flourishing.

We desire to reverse the direction of this decline by emphasizing three principles: freedom, fulfillment, and flourishing. All three of these are biblically grounded and morally right.

MORAL	IMMORAL
Freedom	Bondage and Slavery
Fulfillment	Frustration
Flourishing	Poverty

When we lack political, economic, and religious freedom, we experience bondage and slavery in whole or in part. When we are not free to fulfill our calling, frustration results. When millions of people are not free (in whole or in part) to fulfill their callings, there is poverty.

The biblical view of freedom drives from the inside out. Inner freedom yearns for outer freedom to pursue life without undue obstruction. Political, economic, and religious freedom are not contrary to the biblical perspective. In fact, the biblical perspective is conducive to political, economic, and religious freedom. The rest of this book will show why this is so and why all three are necessary for a flourishing society. The inter-relationships between the three freedoms can be described as a three-legged stool.

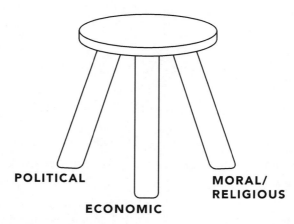

POLITICAL

ECONOMIC

MORAL/ RELIGIOUS

If you damage or eliminate one of the legs of the stool, society becomes unstable, falls over, and fails to flourish. Without political freedom, economic freedom is precarious. It may be maintained for a while, but it is always in danger of being controlled at the whim of the ruling elite. Without economic freedom a society will not flourish. There is a demonstrable relationship between economic freedom and life expectancy, infant mortality, the quality of healthcare, poverty rates, corruption levels, clean environment, civil liberties, income levels, income of the poor, happiness, child labor, and unemployment.[6] The more economically free a society is, the better it performs in all these areas. Another way of saying this is that socialism and Marxism are demonstrably always bad for the poor. This insight from Michael Novak's book, *The Spirit of Democratic Capitalism*, is revolutionary. There are now very extensive yearly reports that demonstrate this, giving detailed surveys of every country in the world, such as the "Economic Freedom of the World Report" and the "Heritage Freedom Index." As these reports indicate, political freedom and economic freedom lead to a flourishing society.

Religiously based moral values – particularly biblical values, are essential, too, for a flourishing society. The third leg of the stool – religious/moral/cultural values – cannot be forgotten. A society will eventually crumble without a solid, religiously-based moral foundation. Political freedom could become anarchy, or a majority of people and their representatives could somehow inexplicably vote for something that is evil. A politically free nation can only rise as high as the character of those involved. Economic freedom without religiously based moral foundation could also be harmful if it is not checked by the rule of law and the informed consciences of those who do business. A lack of religious freedom could lead to a society that refuses to allow the prophetic input of religiously based moral values. Richard Neuhaus argued in his classic book *The Naked Public Square* that such a society could be a disaster.[7]

All these things have been argued in numerous books and articles, and we could profit from rehearsing the things many have discovered. However, in the rest of this book we will try to develop a biblical framework for all three legs of the stool. The Bible does not prescribe a particular form of government or a particular economic system or even a particular view on the (non)establishment of religion. But the biblical perspective does contain principles conducive to political, economic, and religious/moral freedom.

Premise 2: Biblical freedom is based on a moral foundation

The Religious/Moral/Cultural Leg

Our culture was founded on a moral foundation rooted in the Bible. An article in the *Wall Street Journal* titled "In Europe God Is (Not) Dead" notes a prominent thinker's observation:

> Jürgen Habermas, influential German intellectual, member of the originally Marxist Frankfurt School of philosophy and self-described "methodical atheist," has revised his view that modernization inevitably leads to secularization. In a 2004 book, *Time of Transitions*, he hailed Christianity as the bedrock of Western values: "Christianity, and nothing else, is the ultimate foundation of liberty, conscience, human rights, and democracy, the benchmarks of Western civilization. To this day, we have no other options [than Christianity]. We continue to nourish ourselves from this source. Everything else is postmodern chatter."[8]

So many believers and non-believers alike recognize these virtues are uniquely grounded in a biblical framework. It is easy to criticize political and economic freedom, but it is important to note that any criticism of political or economic freedom is inadequate unless it takes into consideration the religious/moral/cultural leg of the stool. There are checks and balances provided on any abuses in the political or economic realm. These freedoms are not in a vacuum, but grounded in the soil of religiously based moral values (i.e., biblical values).

For instance, Austin Hill and Scott Rae argue in their book, *The Virtues of Capitalism,* that there are five core values underlying a market economy: creativity, initiative, cooperation, civility, and responsibility. All five are deeply grounded in biblical roots. Without these virtues, markets cannot flourish.[9]

Similarly, Wayne Grudem and Barry Asmus in their book, *The Poverty of Nations,* list thirty-five biblically based moral virtues that are encouraged by the free enterprise system and in turn help it function. Central to these virtues are honesty and truthfulness, which allow trust to be formed. If a society is so corrupt that people cannot trust and almost every financial contract is violated, then the court system becomes clogged and people will be reluctant or unwilling to do business.

Grudem and Asmus also list a cluster of biblical virtues that are necessary for work and productivity. These virtues include thrift in time or money, doing excellent work (as unto the Lord – Eph. 6:7), using one's creativity to serve others, and developing innovative ways to unlock the potential of God's creation. Biblical values uphold marriage, a necessary condition to addressing poverty.

The biblical worldview teaches that time is linear, meaning that we can learn from the past and have hope for the future. Time is a valuable resource that should not be wasted. We can humbly learn from other nations and will eventually worship God with others from every tribe, tongue, people, and nation (Rev. 7:9).[10]

By emphasizing such values, the Bible provides a foundation essential to free enterprise. Markets viewed from this angle are not "unfettered" or "unbridled." Unless these moral values are deeply rooted in people's conscience and character, free enterprise moves slowly or grinds to a halt. Some have called this capitalism with a conscience, while others have argued for a triple bottom line – people, planet, profit. You might add a fourth value – purpose. Likewise, religiously (biblically) based morality is the only sure foundation for society in general and politics in particular. Peter Kreeft argues:

> Even in a secular society like America it's still true that religion is the firmest support for morality. There has never been a popular secular morality that's lasted and worked in holding a society together. Society has always needed morality, and morality has always needed religion. Destroy religion, you destroy morality; destroy morality, you destroy society. That's history's bottom line.[11]

While this religious/moral/cultural leg is referring primarily to religiously based moral values this is certainly not inconsistent with religious freedom. In fact, believers have good reasons to be at the forefront of defending religious freedom.

First, many of the first settlers in this country left England because their religious liberty was being threatened. You could call religious liberty and tolerance America's first freedom.

Second, we do not believe that you can or ought to physically coerce someone else into religious belief, such as occurred during the Inquisition. We can defend people's legal rights even when we believe them to be wrong. Scripture upholds a right to freedom of conscience even when people's views are misguided (Rom. 14:23).

Third, we have good reason for desiring the non-establishment of religion. Generally, where religion has been established, it has become diluted and weak. Where it has been allowed freedom, it has thrived. Just look at the dwindling established churches (with a few exceptions) in Europe, England, and Scandinavia. Contrast this situation with the vitality (despite many imperfections) of non-established Christianity in America. At the founding of this country (1790), about 10 percent of people attended church once a week.[12] Today, roughly 40 percent attend church in a given week.[13] When there is full freedom to persuade, the most attractive options gain the most adherents. There is a free market of beliefs and ideas.

Fourth, the best way to retain our own freedoms is to be defenders of freedom for others. Leslie Newbigin said:

> If we acknowledge the God of the Bible, we are committed to struggle for justice in society, justice means giving to each his due. Our problem (as seen in light of the gospel) is that each of us overestimates what is due to him as compared with what is due to his neighbor.... If I do not acknowledge a justice which judges the justice for which I fight, I am an agent, not of justice, but of lawless tyranny.[14]

Unless believers become foremost defenders of religious freedom for others as well as themselves, they will not be readily heard when they proclaim the gospel. A precondition for recovering culture is that we are for justice, not "just us."[15]

Religious freedom grows out of this religious/moral/cultural foundation. Again, it is important to emphasize that both a political system and an economic system can only rise as high as the characters of those involved. Religious freedom can only be preserved when rooted in principled character, which is in turn rooted in a biblical foundation.

Political and Economic Freedom

We can certainly give many arguments for the ability of the virtues of political and economic freedom to produce a flourishing society. But can we argue for these two legs biblically? The first step in giving this kind of case is to narrow down our options. Let's take economic freedom first. The three main systems for organizing economies are Marxism, socialism, and free enterprise. Is there any way to exclude the first two biblically? There is, because the Bible clearly teaches the importance of private property and cautions us about the dangers of government that exceeds its bounds. It also teaches us that government's proper role is to protect society from harm. The Bible does not emphasize the provision of goods and services by the state.

In his *Manifesto of the Communist Party*, Karl Marx summarized his central axiom: "The theory of the communists may be summed up in a single sentence: Abolition of private property."[16] Private property is an important biblical principle, and Marxism involves a redistribution of private wealth, so it contradicts biblical teaching. When you add the biblical teaching that leads to a view of limited government, then that would exclude any view that wants to unnecessarily enlarge government. So if private property and limited government are biblical teachings, then Marxism, socialism (large-scale government redistribution of wealth), or big government options are excluded.

We will first sketch the biblical view of private property and then the biblical view of the size and scope of government.

Premise 3: Biblical freedom upholds private property

Private Property

The Bible upholds the importance of owning and being able to use private property. It is especially wrong to steal or to covet someone else's property. Strictly speaking, all property is owned by the Lord. Exodus 19:5 declares that "all the earth is mine,"; Exodus 9:29 that "the earth is the Lord's"; and Leviticus 25:23 that "the land is mine." God is the ultimate owner but has delegated stewardship to his image bearers. He has called them to dominion or rulership over all he has made (Gen. 1:26-28). He carefully preserves the rights of individuals to keep and use their land and property.

For instance, two of the Ten Commandments, "Thou shalt not steal" and "Thou shalt not covet," imply and entail private property (Exod. 20:15, 17, KJV). Stealing involves taking something that is another's. Coveting involves desiring what is another's. Minimally, the prohibition of stealing means that it is wrong to take someone else's property without his or her permission. This prohibition is underlined throughout both the Old and New Testaments.

Divine prohibitions against moving boundary markers occur five times throughout the Old Testament. Deuteronomy 19:14 says, "You shall not move your neighbor's boundary stone which the ancestors have set." This injunction is repeated in Deuteronomy 27:17: "Cursed is he who moves his neighbor's boundary mark." Proverbs 22:28 says, "Do not move the ancient boundary which your fathers have set," and Proverbs 23:10 warns, "Do not move the ancient boundary or go into the fields of the fatherless." In a list of those that do evil, Job 24:2 includes: "Some remove the landmarks; they seize and devour flocks."

The story of the prophet Elijah's rebuke of Ahab and Jezebel for the murder of Naboth and their acquisition of his vineyard is a classic biblical story of theft. King Ahab saw Naboth's vineyard, which was close to his own, and coveted it. Ahab offered either to exchange another vineyard for Naboth's or to buy it from him. Naboth firmly refused, saying, "The Lord forbid me that I should give you the inheritance of my fathers" (1 Kings 21:3).

Jezebel found Ahab sulking on his bed after this disappointment and devised a plan to kill Naboth and steal his land. She proposed a feast with Naboth as the guest of honor, "at the head of the people" (1 Kings 21:9). During the feast, "worthless men" would be seated around him to accuse him of cursing God and the king. The plan was executed, and it succeeded. Naboth was stoned, and Ahab acquired his coveted vineyard. Elijah, however, pronounced severe judgment on Ahab and Jezebel for this wicked deed.

This prohibition against stealing was not, of course, unique to the ancient Jews. Old Testament scholar Walter Kaiser notes that "Rome made this crime one that was punishable by death, so seriously did they view such an action."[17]

Christianity inherited this prohibition:

- In the New Testament, Jesus reiterates some of the Ten Commandments to the rich young ruler, including "Do not steal" (Mark 10:9; Luke 18:20).

- After meeting Jesus, Zacchaeus promises fourfold restitution to those he has defrauded (Luke 19:8).

- In Romans, Paul argues that the eighth commandment is part of what it means to love your neighbor as yourself (Rom. 13:9).

- In 1 Corinthians 6:9-10, Paul lists habitual thieves as those who will not inherit the kingdom of God. Paul clearly states, "He who steals must steal no longer; but rather he must labor, performing with his own hands what is good, so that he will have something to share with one who has need" (Eph. 4:28).

Christians have accepted the biblical prohibition against theft and have continued to work out its implications. According to Kaiser, "John Calvin found removing the boundary stone to be an act of double deceit, for it was both an act of theft and one of false witness."[18] It is evident that the New Testament restates emphatically the prohibition of theft, which clearly implies the upholding of private property. If private property is moral and biblical, then Marxism is immoral and unbiblical.

Premise 4: Biblical freedom limits government power

Limited Government

We need to have freedom within the structure of law, enforced by government. But when government becomes too intrusive, we lose freedom. The debate about the size and role of government has huge implications for the lives of individuals all over the world. Important as the issue is, Christians are divided about what Scripture has to say about government. Some, such as J.P. Moreland, argue that the Bible teaches limited government, and Doug Bandow points to the biblical foundations of this idea.[19] Others maintain that the Bible is consistent with big government of some sort.[20] What are some considerations that can help us frame this debate and work toward a conclusion?

1. GOVERNMENT IS ESTABLISHED BY GOD.

Romans 13:1-7 is the *locus classicus* on the topic of government. E.F. Harrison calls it "the most notable passage in the New Testament on Christian civic responsibility."[21] Verse 1 says that "there is no authority except from God, and those which exist are established by God. Therefore he who resists authority has opposed the ordinance of God." This is a strong endorsement of the intrinsic goodness of government, in its proper role. This endorsement is reinforced in verse 4: "for [the authority] is a minister of God to you for good. But if you do what is evil, be afraid; for it does not bear the sword for nothing; for it is a minister of God, an avenger who brings wrath on the one who practices evil." Verse 6 calls rulers "servants of God." John Murray says, "This designation removes every supposition to the effect that magistracy is per se evil and serves good only in the sense that as a lesser evil it restrains and counteracts greater evils."[22]

This, of course, does not mean that all government actions are right. Note that the term used in verses 1 and 5 is "subjection," not "obey." Harrison comments:

> What he requires is submission, a term that calls for placing one's self under someone else. Here and in verse 5 he seems to avoid using the stronger word "obey," and the reason is that the believer may find it impossible to comply with every demand of government. A circumstance may arise in which he must choose between obeying God and obeying men (Acts 5:29). But even then he must be submissive to the extent that if his Christian convictions do not permit his compliance, he will accept the consequences of his refusal.[23]

If the government forbids what God commands (such as prayer in Daniel 6) or commands what God forbids (such as idolatry in Daniel 3), then the believer must disobey human authority and pay the consequences.[24]

2. GOVERNMENT'S ROLE IS MORE NEGATIVE THAN POSITIVE.

In its proper role, government punishes or exercises vengeance on the evildoer, according to several passages in the New Testament. Paul's description of government in Romans 13:4 stands in contrast to the believer's personal response to evil in the passage immediately preceding. Romans 12:17 commands believers to "never...pay back evil for evil," and verse 19 says, "Never take your own revenge, beloved, but leave room for the wrath of God, for it is written, 'Vengeance is mine, I will repay says the Lord.'" Individuals are not to avenge themselves but turn the task of vengeance over to God. We are to "overcome evil with good" and to do good to our enemies, giving them food or drink when necessary (Rom. 12:20-21). This passage echoes the Sermon on the Mount: "Love your enemies" (Matt. 5:44). God is not ignoring or forgetting the injustice. Rather, he will exercise vengeance in his own time as well as use the government to do his task. John Murray comments, "Thus the magistrate is the avenger in executing the judgment that accrues to the evildoer from the wrath of God."[25] God has appointed government as one of his instruments of justice.

To borrow a term from political theory, the government that punishes evil in Romans 13:4 is playing a negative role. Government plays a negative role when it protects a citizen in his or her own pursuit of something legitimate; by punishing evil, the government plays a negative role because it is protecting a citizen's own pursuit of private property, health, and life. In contrast, government plays a positive role when it directly provides something to its citizens.

The latter part of Romans 13:4 emphasizes government's negative role: "It is a minister of God," bearing the sword—the power to coerce or kill— "an avenger who brings wrath on the one who practices evil." Verse 3 says, "Do what is good and you will have praise from the same [authority]." In this passage, government is not called to do the good or to play a positive role by creating rights, goods, or services, but to give praise to those who do good. This praise could involve special recognition for those who serve in exemplary ways or just acknowledgment, official or otherwise, for being a good citizen. Murray says, "The praise could be expressed by saying that good behavior secures good standing in the state, a status to be cherished and cultivated."[26] This passage does not prohibit government from providing goods and services but strongly puts the emphasis on upholding rule of law and encouraging good behavior. This passage alone certainly would not give warrant to those who want a big government.

Similarly, 1 Peter 2:13-14 says, "Submit yourselves for the Lord's sake to every human institution; whether to a king or one in authority, or to governors as sent by him for the punishment of evildoers and the praise of those who do right." Note again that this summary of government's role gives primacy to the rule of law, or punishing evil. It is also to give praise to those who do right, rather than doing the good itself. The accent is on government's negative role, not on a positive role of doing good deeds or providing for people.

Jesus rejected the political pathway to inaugurate his coming kingdom, and today's Christians should as well. He said that his "kingdom is not of this world" (John 18:36). Jesus acknowledged Caesar's place ("give to Caesar what is Caesar's") and God's place ("give to God what is God's"). (Matt. 22:20-22). Tim Keller says the following on these words of Jesus:

> This was the very first theory of limited government in the history of the world.... Give Caesar the money because it's his money—he printed it—but don't give him the allegiance.... What Jesus Christ is saying is that you may give Caesar some of what he wants, which is his money, but you cannot give Caesar ultimately what he wants, which is to completely accept his system of coercion, his system of injustice, his system of exclusion—he wants ultimate allegiance, he wants no one to sit in judgment on him, but we can't give him that.[27]

When standing before Pilate, Jesus acknowledged Pilate's authority over him, but said, "You would have no authority over Me, unless it had been given you from above" (John 19:11). Perhaps this is the root from which Paul developed his teaching in Romans 13.

Another indicative passage is 1 Timothy 2:1-2: "I urge that prayers... be made...for kings and all who are in authority in order that they may live a tranquil and quiet life in all godliness and dignity." Note that the prayers are for the authorities—secular kings—to provide a rule of law so that there might be safety and security. J.P. Moreland says this passage calls for prayers to "sustain stable social order in which people can live peacefully and quietly without fear of harm."[28]

The above passages are so important because they set forth the New Testament perspective toward secular government. The Old Testament had established a theocracy where Israelite kings were expected to adhere to the

Old Testament law. Today, however, most people live in societies more similar to the pagan nations found Amos 1 and 2, rather than in societies similar to Israel. Moreland argues that the biblical laws for Israel are more applicable to the modern day Church than to the secular government. He points out,

> The prophet chastises these [pagan] nations and rulers for violating people's negative rights, e.g., for forced deportation of a population, torturing and killing pregnant women, stealing, forced slavery, and murder. There is no expectation in the passage that the nations and rulers were to provide positive rights for people. This is typical of the prophets and their understanding of the responsibilities of pagan rulers and nations.[29]

3. BIBLICAL WARNINGS ABOUT GOVERNMENT.

From Genesis to Revelation, the Bible is full of examples and warnings of abusive government. In Genesis and the beginning of Exodus, this is evident in Egypt where the Pharaoh initially resists Moses's plea to "let my people go" (Exod. 9). We see in Pharaoh a hard-hearted totalitarian tyrant resisting submission even after several plagues show God's power. Passover is a celebration that commemorates prophetic resistance to a totalitarian dictator and God's powerful deliverance of his people from slavery (Exod. 12). It is a defining moment in the Old Testament.

At times, people longed for a king. After Gideon's victory, the Israelites wanted to make him king and set up a dynasty so that his sons would continue the rule. But Gideon said, "I will not rule over you, nor my son rule over you; the Lord shall rule over you" (Judg. 8:23). Later when Samuel's sons, his successors, became corrupt and resorted to taking bribes from the people, the Israelites again cried out for a king to judge them and defend them against warring nations. They wanted a king "like all the nations" (1 Sam. 8:5). God told Samuel to listen to the people even though it meant rejecting God's kingship. Bill Arnold, in his commentary on 1 and 2 Samuel, argues that the Israelite demand for a king was "sinful in its motive, selfish in its timing, and cowardly in its spirit." The Israelites were seeking conformity and security. What they failed to see was that unchecked kings would "become militaristic, conscript Israelite men, confiscate property, and lead ultimately to enslavement."[30]

Samuel told the people that kings would "take" their sons for their armies, "take" their daughters for cooks and bakers, "take" the best of their fields, "take" a tenth of their seed and their vineyards, "take" their best young men, "take" a tenth of their flock. Eventually, he warned, "you yourselves will become [the king's] servants" (1 Sam. 8:10-17). Samuel predicted that the king would take so much that "you will cry out in that day because of the king whom you have chosen for yourselves" (1 Sam. 8:18). Arnold sums up this passage as follows: "The theme words of Samuel's warnings are 'take' and 'serve'.... Nothing seems beyond the grasp of the king, whether children, personal property, or one's freedom. Kings take and take and when everything is gone they force you to serve. The final indignation: 'you yourselves will become his slaves.'"[31]

The history of kings in the Old Testament reveals that most were, in fact, "takers." Even Solomon, who started so well, "did what was evil in the sight of the Lord and did not follow the Lord fully" (1 Sam. 11:6). He did not listen to the Deuteronomic warning to future kings: "He shall not multiply horses for himself.... neither shall he multiply wives for himself, lest his heart turn away; nor shall he greatly increase silver and gold for himself" (Deut. 17:16-17). Yet Solomon did all these things, even establishing centers for idolatrous worship for his foreign wives. Proverbs 19:28, ascribed to Solomon, says, "Cease listening, my son, to discipline, and you will stray from the words of knowledge." He started well but failed to remember his own advice.

Solomon also heavily taxed the people. After Solomon's death, his son Rehoboam rose to power. The elders of Israel came to Rehoboam and pleaded that he might "lighten the hard service of your father and his heavy yoke which he put on us" (1 Kings 12:4). The king rejected the advice of his elders that he should listen to the people and took the advice of young friends who grew up with him. He responded to the elders of Israel, "My father made your yoke heavy, but I will add to your yoke; my father disciplined you with whips, but I will discipline you with scorpions" (1 Kings 12:14). This misjudgment led to the division of the kingdom and a rejection of Rehoboam's authority. Rehoboam refused to limit his power and greatly miscalculated, losing about half his kingdom.

Although kingship is not intrinsically bad, the history of this type of government reflects the Fall and the truth of Lord Acton's proverb: "Power corrupts and absolute power corrupts absolutely."[32] Time after time, governments in the Old Testament exceeded their bounds, clearly reflecting the need for government to be limited. The examples of Pharaoh, Samuel's warning about the dangers of kingship, Solomon's excess, and Rehoboam's folly are just a few examples from the Old Testament demonstrating the need for government to respect limits to its power. Many more examples exist, some of which Tom Pratt highlights in his paper.[33] Perhaps the most dramatic usurpation of power occurs in Revelation 13:1-10. In this vision, John sees a beast rising out of the sea and gaining great power and authority. One leader, seemingly resurrected from the dead, speaks "arrogant words." He attacks believers and gains authority over "every tribe and people and tongue and nation." All except true believers worship him. Leon Morris says, "Hendriksen sees the beast as signifying worldly government directed against the Church and he takes to a multiplicity of heads to indicate that this has various forms as Babylon, Assyria, Rome, etc."[34]

Some commentators think that the beast is Rome. It may be, but it also signifies more than Rome, perhaps pointing to the future. Robert Mounce comments,

> The worship of the satanically-inspired perversion of secular authority is the ultimate offense against the one true God. The temptation rejected by Jesus at the outset of his public ministry [Matthew 4:8-10] reappears at the end of history in its most persuasive form and gains the allegiance of all but the elect.[35]

God has clearly approved of government as an authority. God chooses to use government as a tool in order to uphold order, justice, and the rule of law.

Thus, believers are to respect and pray for their leaders while submitting themselves to the authority provided by the government. Yet government itself is composed of fallen individuals and is far from perfect. As a result, Scripture makes clear that God has also placed limits and expectations on the government. In the Old Testament, for instance, Israelite kings were expected to obey God's laws as written in the Pentateuch.

Now that most governments are not theocratic but secular, Christians must concern themselves with where they can have influence to make sure that government does not grow beyond its bounds. The Bible provides many examples of government that grew to become oppressive, and Christians must be vigilant lest those in authority take, take, and take ever more. According to Romans 13:7, it is certainly right to pay taxes. Yet in the words of John Calvin, rulers "should remember that all they receive from people is public property, and not a means of satisfying private lust and luxury."[36]

Perhaps the whole debate on limited government is between Romans 13 and Revelation 13. Government has its God-ordained place but can easily become tyrannical. In Romans, we see the negative role of government to stop evil by upholding the rule of law. In Revelation, we see government taking over all, including worship. The Bible repeatedly provides examples of governments that became corrupt and usurped freedom, property, and money. In addition, these and many governments today are highly bureaucratic, impersonal, inefficient, and often not grounded on biblical principles. The larger they become, the more resources they require from their citizens. These considerations might lead many to question whether government should play a positive role in providing goods and services. It might be helpful to ask first whether churches, nonprofits, private enterprise, and other non-government institutions could provide these goods and services more efficiently, economically, and wisely.

These arguments point to a need for limited government. But the question remains, how limited? If Romans 13:1-7 and 1 Peter 2:13-14 are to be our guide, then government should be limited to the negative: punishing evil.

It could be argued that just because Scripture does not command a government to play a positive role, it does not forbid it either. However, in light of the considerations discussed above, the burden of proof lies with advocates of government expansion, since this involves relying so extensively upon the resources of others and raises the specter of power's tendency to corrupt those who wield it.

Ultimately, when coming to a conclusion about the size and scope of government, Christians must carefully assess the consequences of their choices, listening to biblical warnings, pondering the pervasiveness of the Fall, and learning from the lessons of history.[37]

The Bible does teach the importance of private property, which rules out Marxism as a biblical option. The Bible teaches limited government, repeatedly warning about the danger of government abuse in the Scriptures cited above, which excludes socialism and big government alternatives. The bigger government becomes, the less free we become. This bears consequences for creativity and innovation.

Premise 5: Biblical freedom and innovation

Creativity

The biblical pillars of private property and limited government steer us away from Marxism and socialism. There is freedom of private ownership and freedom from undue government intrusion. But can we say more about what path we should pursue?

The freer we are to use our gifts, the more we will be fulfilled. When millions of people are using their creative gifts in society, there is also flourishing. Remember the chart referenced earlier.

MORAL	IMMORAL
Freedom	Bondage and Slavery
Fulfillment	Frustration
Flourishing	Poverty

If there is not freedom, there is relative or absolute bondage or slavery. When there is not fulfillment, there is frustration. When society is not flourishing, there is poverty. This freedom to use our creativity is grounded in the image of God and the cultural mandate.

Genesis 1:26-28 has been called the cultural mandate because it shows the place of human beings in creation and calls us to work with the things God has made, ruling over, clarifying, reshaping, developing, and unfolding the potential which we have been given. It is a key to knowing who we are and what we are to do. Genesis 1:26-28 reads:

> Then God said, "Let us make men in our own image according to our likeness, and let them rule over the fish of the sea, and over the birds of the sky, and over the cattle and over all the earth, and over every creeping thing that creeps on the earth." God created man in His own image, in the image of God He created them; male and female He created them. God blessed them; and God said to them, "Be fruitful and multiply, and fill the earth, and subdue it; and rule over the fish of the sea and over the birds of the sky and over every living thing that moves on the earth."

First, being made in the image of God, we have intrinsic worth, value, and dignity. This passage twice reiterates that humans are made in the image and likeness of God. James 3:9 rebukes those who would worship God with their mouths and then walk out the next moment and curse someone who is made in the likeness of God. What hypocrisy! When Christians bless God but curse those made in his image, they contradict themselves. They are failing to see the connection between the worthiness of God and the worth of people. C.S. Lewis wrote, "There are no *ordinary* people. You have never talked to a mere mortal. Nations, cultures, arts, civilization—these are mortal, and their life is to ours as the life of a gnat."[38] The evangelical church has yet to realize the implications of the image of God for personal and public life. Suffice it to say that the dignity, worth, and value of every person you see each day is more important than you presently know.

The first task to which image bearers of God are called is to "rule" over the creation. God is the king, but we are the vice-regents. He is the creator, but human beings are sub-creators. Only God can make something out of nothing. But humans are called to create something out of something. We can take wood and make a table or a house. We can take metal and make a tool or a musical instrument. We can take stone and make a statue or a wall. There are endless options we can use to develop the potential in the creation. Creativity (rulership, dominion) is the central calling of humans from the beginning of creation. Although the Fall makes our tasks more difficult, working by the sweat of our brows through thorns and thistles (Gen. 3:17-19), this central call to creativity is not canceled.

After the Fall, humans used their creativity to fulfill the cultural mandate. Very soon people were making musical instruments and many things from bronze and iron (Gen. 4:22). In his commentary on Genesis, Calvin describes this ongoing creativity as from the Spirit:

> For the invention of the arts, and of other things which serve to the common use and convenience of life, is a gift from God by no means to be despised, and a faculty worthy of commendation . . . as the experience of all ages teaches us how widely the rays of divine light have shone on unbelieving nations, for the benefit of the present life; and we see, at the present time, that the excellent gifts of the Spirit are diffused through the whole human race.[39]

This creativity that is so central to our humanness is best developed in a society where there is freedom. We need to be free to develop new creative products, new businesses, new forms of expression. Where there is heavy-handed government, this creativity wanes. I visited Eastern Europe and the former Soviet Union immediately after the wall came down (in 1990 and 1991). You could see and feel the effects of Marxism on people and on buildings, businesses, and cultures. For instance, in Odessa, Ukraine, when we went into a store, employees just sat there. There was no desire to serve, no willingness to even complete a sale. People's spirits were crushed. Trust was non-existent. Initiative was lacking. The most common phrase was, "It is impossible."

Creativity is also sapped by socialist societies or those societies with many government regulations. For instance, Hernando de Soto in his groundbreaking book, *The Mystery of Capital,* discusses the frustration people in many countries experience when trying to buy land or start a business. De Soto says that the procedure to formalize property in the Philippines could:

> Necessitate 168 steps involving 53 public and private agencies and taking thirteen to twenty-five years.... In Egypt, the person who wants to acquire and legally register a lot on state owned desert land must work his way through at least 77 bureaucratic procedures at thirty-one public and private agencies.... This can take anywhere from five to fourteen years.... Total time to gain lawful land in Haiti: nineteen years.... Yet even this ordeal will not ensure that the property remains legal.[40]

Starting a business in these countries can be just as difficult and frustrating. For instance, de Soto and his team tried to open a small garment shop with one worker in Lima, Peru. The team worked six hours a day, and it still took 289 days. The cost was about three years' salary.[41]

When people are not able to own and use their property and not able to use their creativity to start businesses, their humanity is diminished. Only where there is freedom to be creative upheld by the rule of law, a protection of private property, and an encouragement of creative expression are countries able to flourish.

As Christians, our view of these things is influenced by the story of Creation and the principles of human nature, particularly our call to creativity, that it presents. If Creation influences our view of freedom, so must the Fall.

Premise 6: Biblical freedom always considers the Fall

We must beware of idealistic or utopian solutions to our society's ills. We must remember that the Fall permeates every area of personal and public life. Life is far from perfect, as we well know. This is true not only in our marriages, families, schools, and work, but in our political and economic systems. We might ask, what political and economic systems are the ablest to address our fallen situation? Certainly a full answer would have to be book length. But perhaps a couple observations might be remembered as we think about these things.

Winston Churchill once said, "Democracy is the worst form of government, except for all those other forms that have been tried from time to time."[42] In the U.S., the rejection of the concentration of power in one individual or even in one branch of government shows skepticism about possible abuses of power. There are "checks and balances" or a "balance of powers." At least in theory, the legislative branch (the House and the Senate) is to check the executive branch (the President), and the judicial branch (the Supreme Court) is to check the other two. This system makes it more difficult for evil to gain a foothold though, alas, it makes it harder for good to be achieved as well. The legislative process delays, dilutes, and sometimes prevents the best plans from succeeding. Nevertheless, it is good that people are called to be in such positions. Without them, the situation would be much worse. Thomas Aquinas maintained that the best form of government would be Kingship, but only if you had a perfectly good and wise king. He also realized it would be the worst form of government if that king was wicked. A democratic system such as we have in the USA protects freedom and restrains evil.

Economic freedom is also precarious. Marxism seeks to control the economy and socialism seeks to severely restrict the marketplace. In the latter case, there is a desire to protect people from real (or imagined) abuses. But in the process of doing this there are (perhaps) unintended consequences – power is concentrated in government, freedom is restricted, and flourishing lessened. This protection is sometimes considered to be progress, but given these outcomes, we must ask, "progress in which direction?"

Premise 7: Biblical freedom encourages toward true progress

In a day when some politicians try to be "more progressive than thou," we need to consider what kind of future we want to see and what kind of progress we want to make.

Perhaps it would be valuable to conclude this book with a reflection from C.S. Lewis's writing on the nature of good and bad progress.

C.S. Lewis warned that we cannot give a blank check to "progress" in itself. After all, some progress leads to sickness rather than health.

A story from *The Voyage of the Dawn Treader*, the fifth book in *The Chronicles of Narnia* series, illustrates the wrong kind of progress.[43] In the book, King Caspian encounters Gumpas, the Governor of the Lone Islands. Gumpas tells Caspian that the slave trade practiced in his domain is an "essential part of the development of the island." Caspian objects to the practice. Gumpas counters his objections by claiming that all the economic indicators prove his case and that he has the statistics and graphs to back it up.

"Tender as my years may be," says Caspian, "I do not see that it brings into the islands meat or bread or beer or wine or timber or cabbages or books or instruments of music or horses or armour or anything else worth having. But whether it does or not, it must be stopped."

"But that would be putting the clock back," gasps the governor. "Have you no idea of progress, of development?"

"I have seen them both in an egg," says Caspian. "We call it going bad in Narnia. This trade must stop."

Caspian's response reflects Lewis's contention that not all progress is good. The newly-developed slave trade was an example of "progress" in a direction that would lead to rottenness.

Sometimes we need to go back in order to go forward. G.K. Chesterton said, "Real development is not leaving things behind, as on a road, but drawing life from them as from a root." Though some would object that looking backward for wisdom is like turning back the clock to an earlier century, Lewis answers this objection in his book, *Mere Christianity*:

We all want progress. But progress means getting nearer to the place you want to be and if you have taken a wrong turning, then to go forward does not get you any nearer. If you are on the wrong road, progress means doing an about-turn and walking back to the right road; and in that case, the man who turns back soonest is the most progressive man. We have all seen this when we do arithmetic. When I have started a sum the wrong way, the sooner I admit this and go back and start over again, the faster I shall get on. There is nothing progressive about being pigheaded and refusing to admit a mistake. And I think if you look at the present state of the world, it is pretty plain that humanity has been making some big mistakes. We are on the wrong road. And if that is so, we must go back. Going back is the quickest way on.[44]

Certainly it is never wise to go back to the past simply for its own sake. The past sometimes shows us how to live and sometimes how not to live. The classic proverb holds true: If we do not learn from history's mistakes, we are bound to repeat them.

C.S. Lewis was not afraid to be called old-fashioned or outdated. In "De Descriptione Temporium," his inaugural address to his professorship at Cambridge,[45] Lewis claimed to be more a part of the old Western order than the present post-Christian one. He acknowledged that while his outlook might seem to disqualify him from having anything important to say, it could also be a positive qualification. He admitted, "You don't want to be lectured on…dinosaurs by a dinosaur." On the other hand, Lewis suggested that, "Where I fail as a critic, I may be useful as a specimen. I would dare to go further…I would say, use your specimen while you can. There are not going to be many more dinosaurs."

Lewis also had a great deal to say about "progress" in economics and politics, even though he did not often comment on these topics. When he was invited by the *Observer* in the late 1950's to write an article on whether progress was even possible, he entitled his contribution "Is Progress Possible?: Willing Slaves of the Welfare State."[46] The title itself indicates his sobering message.

In the essay, he encourages progress in "increasing the goodness and happiness of individual lives." He adds, however, "Progress means movement in a desired direction and we do not all desire the same things for our species."

Lewis is particularly concerned about the tendencies in the UK during World Wars I and II to give up liberty for security. He says we have grown "though apparently grudgingly, accustomed to our chains." He warns that once government encroaches on our freedom, every concession makes it more difficult for us to "retrace our steps." Perhaps the most striking quotation from this essay is the one on the nature of the happiness that he would like to see. Lewis says:

> I believe a man is happier, and happy in a richer way, if he has 'the freeborn mind.' But I doubt whether he can have this without economic independence, which the new society is abolishing. For independence allows an education not controlled by Government; and in adult life it is the man who needs and asks nothing of Government who can criticize its acts and snap his fingers at its ideology. Read Montaigne; that's the voice of a man with his legs under his own table, eating the mutton and turnips raised on his own land. Who will talk like that when the State is everyone's schoolmaster and employer?

Note Lewis's desire for freedom, economic and political. This economic "independence" allows free people to eat their own "mutton and turnips." This echoes the classic passage in Micah 4:4 which says that "each of them will sit under his vine and under his fig tree with no one to make them afraid."

Lewis is especially concerned about the advent of a worldwide welfare state and sees the enticement to accept it. Giving up freedom for security is a "terrible bargain" that is so tempting that "we cannot blame men for making it. We can hardly wish them not to. Yet we can hardly bear that they should." Despite the temptation, if people do make this bargain, the loss of freedom will lead to "total frustration" and "disastrous results, both moral and psychological."

The temptation to turn our destiny over to the state often ignores the realization that some will take charge of others. These will simply be men and women, "none perfect; some greedy, cruel, and dishonest." The more that people in government control our lives, the more we have to ask "why, this time power should not corrupt as it always has done before?"

Lewis believes that we should be progressive if it leads to greater happiness. Sometimes, however, we need to go back in order to go forward, turning the "clock back" or doing an about-face on the wrong road in order to find the right one. We should not be afraid of being called outdated, old-fashioned, or even a "dinosaur."

Sometimes we need to go full-speed astern in order to go forward. If we see that we have begun wrongly, we must start all over. In personal life, this means repentance. In public life, it means protecting our freedoms and pushing back against the power of the "welfare state," lest we be increasingly constrained in our ability to choose what we want to do and be. We all want progress, to be true progressives, but that means something different than what we hear in the culture. We need to pursue progress that leads toward biblical freedom.

CONCLUSION

In this chapter we have seen that:

1. Political, economic, and religious freedom are dependent on each other.

2. Biblical freedom is based on a moral foundation.

3. Biblical freedom upholds private property.

4. Biblical freedom limits government power.

5. Biblical freedom encourages creativity and innovation.

6. Biblical freedom always considers the Fall.

7. Biblical freedom encourages true progress.

There is a desperate need for a preservation (and recovery) of political, economic, and religious freedom within a context of biblical morality. There is also the need for government to protect that freedom. Government's primary role is to punish people who do evil – and especially to protect life and property. There may be a place for a government safety net where the church or non-profits are not able to meet specific needs. But we must beware of government taking, taking, and taking even more. We don't want to entrust our lives to a godless, impersonal, inefficient, bureaucratic, uneconomical entity. It is much better if our solutions to human needs are godly, personal (local), efficient, and economically viable.

The future of the U.S. and other nations depends on the degree to which we preserve our freedoms. There is a biblical basis for freedom and numerous guidelines for choosing between political and economic alternatives. May we choose wisely and encourage others in that pursuit.

ABOUT THE AUTHOR
ART LINDSLEY, PHD

Rev. Dr. Art Lindsley is the vice president of theological initiatives at the Institute, where he oversees the development of a theology that integrates faith, work, and economics. Most recently, he has served as the president and senior fellow at the C.S. Lewis Institute since 1987. Prior to that, he was the director of educational ministries at the Ligonier Valley Study Center and staff specialist with the Coalition of Christian Outreach in Pittsburgh, Pennsylvania.

He is an editor of and contributing author to IFWE's recently released book, *For the Least of These: A Biblical Answer to Poverty*. In his chapter, Rev. Dr. Lindsley walks through Leviticus 25 to explain common myths about Jubilee. He also examines claims that Acts chapters 2 through 5 teach socialism and demonstrates how these claims are incorrect.

He is also the author of *C.S. Lewis's Case for Christ*, *True Truth*, and *Love: The Ultimate Apologetic*. He is co-author with R.C. Sproul and John Gerstner of *Classical Apologetics*, and he often writes articles on theology, apologetics, C.S. Lewis, and the lives of many other authors and teachers.

Rev. Dr. Lindsley earned his bachelor of science in chemistry from Seattle Pacific University, master of divinity from Pittsburgh Theological Seminary, and doctor of philosophy in religious studies from the University of Pittsburgh. Rev. Dr. Lindsley, his wife Connie, and their two boys Trey and Jonathan make their home in Arlington, VA.

ABOUT THE INSTITUTE
FOR FAITH, WORK & ECONOMICS

The Institute for Faith, Work & Economics™ (IFWE) is a nonprofit, 501(c)(3) Christian research organization committed to promoting biblical and economic principles that help individuals find fulfillment in their work and contribute to a free and flourishing society.

IFWE's research starts with the belief that the Bible, as the inerrant Word of God, provides the authoritative and intellectual foundation for a proper understanding of work and economic truths that, when properly followed, can help individuals, companies, communities, and nations flourish.

IFWE's research is based on three core principles:

1. Each person is created in God's image and, like him, has a desire to be creative and to find **fulfillment** using their God-given talents through work.

2. All work, whether paid or volunteer, matters to God, and we as Christians are called to pursue excellence throughout the week—not just on Sundays—stewarding all that we've been given for God's glory and for the **flourishing** of society.

3. Therefore, we as citizens must promote an economic environment that not only provides us the **freedom** to pursue our callings and flourish in our work but also reflects the inherent dignity of every human being.

Our desire is to help Christians view their work within the bigger picture of what God is doing in the world. Not only do we help Christians find personal fulfillment, but we also help them understand how to better alleviate poverty, address greed, and view possessions properly. With a biblical view of work and economics, we can partner together to be meaningful participants in God's plan to restore the world to the way he intended it to be.

ENDNOTES

1. Kittel, Gerhard and Friedrich, Gerhard, eds. *Theological Dictionary of the New Testament.* William B. Eerdmans Publishing Company: Grand Rapids, MI, 1985, p. 224.

2. Calvin, John. *Commentary on the Gospel of John,* Vol. I, Baker Book House: Grand Rapids, MI, 1989, p. 342.

3. Davids, Peter. On James 2:12. *New International Biblical Commentary.* Hendrickson Publishers: Peabody, MA, p. 74.

4. Motyer, J.A. *The Tests of Faith,* InterVarsity Press: London, 1972, p. 36.

5. Dreisbach, Daniel L. "'The Vine and Fig Tree' in George Washington's Letters: Reflections on a Biblical Motif in the Literature of the American Founding Era" *Anglican and Episcopal History* 76, no. 3 (September 2007), p. 322.

6. Anne Bradley and Joe Connors, "Economic Freedom and the Path to Flourishing." http://ifwe.s3.amazonaws.com/wp-content/uploads/2015/07/Economic-Freedom-and-the-Path-.pdf

7. Richard John Neuhaus, *The Naked Public Square: Religion and Democracy in America* (Grand Rapids, MI: Eerdmans, 1988).

8. Higgins, Andrew. "In Europe God Is (Not) Dead." *Wall Street Journal,* July 14, 2007. http://www.wsj.com/articles/SB118434936941966055.

9. Austin Hill and Scott Rae, *The Virtues of Capitalism: A Moral Case for Free Markets* (Chicago, IL: Northfield Publishing, 2010), 41-55.

10. Barry Asmus and Wayne Grudem, *The Poverty of Nations: A Sustainable Solution* (Wheaton, IL: Crossway, 2013), 322-324.

11. Peter Kreeft, *A Refutation of Moral Relativism: Interviews with an Absolutist* (San Francisco, CA: Ignatius Press, 1999), 162.

12. Mark C. Carnes, John A. Garrety, and Patrick Williams, *Mapping America's Past: A Historical Atlas* (New York: Henry Holt and Company, 1996), 50.

13. Frank Newport, "In U.S., Four in 10 Report Attending Church Last Week," *Gallup,* December 24, 2013, http://www.gallup.com/poll/166613/four-report-attending-church-last-week.aspx.

14. Lesslie Newbigin, *The Open Secret: Sketches for a Missionary Theology* (Grand Rapids, MI: Eerdmans, 1978), 124.

15. Lindsley, *True Truth,* 23-33.

16. Karl Marx and Friedrich Engels, *Marx/Engels Selected Works,* vol. 1, (Progress Publishers, Moscow, 1969), pp. 98-137, accessed at https://www.marxists.org/archive/marx/works/1848/communist-manifesto/ch02.htm, accessed September 3, 2014.

17. Walter C. Kaiser, Jr., "Ownership and Property in the Old Testament Economy," http://tifwe.org/resources/ownership-and-property-in-the-old-testament-economy/, accessed September 3, 2014.

18. Kaiser, "Ownership and Property."

19. J.P. Moreland, "A Biblical Case for Limited Government," Institute for Faith, Work, and Economics, http://tifwe.org/research/a-biblical-case-for-limited-government/, accessed July 26, 2013; Doug Bandow, "Biblical Foundations of Limited Government," http://tifwe.org/resources/biblical-foundations-of-limited-government/, accessed July 26, 2013.

20. Art Lindsley, "Does Acts 2-5 Teach Socialism?" Institute for Faith, Work & Economics, http://tifwe.org/research/does-acts-2-5-teach-socialism/, accessed July 26, 2013.

21. E. F. Harrison, The Expositor's Bible Commentary, vol. 10 (Grand Rapids, MI: Zondervan, 1976), 136.

22. John Murray, Romans (Grand Rapids, MI: Eerdmans, 1968), 152.

23. Harrison, 136-7.

24. There is even a place for just revolution in extreme circumstances. For a good treatment of this issue, see John Jefferson Davis's book Evangelical Ethics (Phillipsburg, NJ: Presbyterian and Reformed Publishing, 2004), chapter 10.

25. Murray, 153.

26. Ibid., 151.

27. Timothy Keller, "Arguing About Politics" (sermon, Redeemer Presbyterian Church, New York, NY, July 15, 2001), http://sermons2.redeemer.com/sermons/arguing-about-politics, accessed September 3, 2014.

28. Moreland, "A Biblical Case for Limited Government."

29. Ibid.

30. Bill Arnold, The NIV Application Commentary: 1 and 2 Samuel (Grand Rapids, MI: Zondervan, 2003), 149.

31. Ibid., 151.

32. Lord Acton, "Acton-Creighton Correspondence [1887]," Online Library of Liberty, http://oll.libertyfund.org/titles/acton-acton-creighton-correspondence#lf1524_label_010, accessed September 3, 2014.

33. Tom Pratt, "God and Government: A Biblical Perspective," The Institute for Faith, Work & Economics, http://tifwe.org/research/god-and-government-a-biblical-perspective-the-bible-and-limited-government/, accessed July 26, 2013.

34. Leon Morris, Revelation (Grand Rapids, MI: Eerdmans, 2002), 161.

35. Robert Mounce, Revelation (Grand Rapids, MI: Eerdmans, 1977), 255.

36. John Calvin, Calvin's New Testament Commentaries: Romans and Thessalonians (Grand Rapids, MI: Eerdmans, 1995), 284.

37. For an in-depth discussion about these "lessons of history," see Chad Brand's "A Case for Limited Government," Institute for Faith, Work & Economics, http://tifwe.org/research/limited-government-2/, accessed July 26, 2013.

38. C.S. Lewis, The Weight of Glory (New York: HarperOne, 2001), 45-46.

39. John Calvin, Commentaries on the First Book of Moses Called Genesis, Vol. 1 (Grand Rapids, MI: Baker, 1996)

40. Hernando de Soto, The Mystery of Capital: Why Capitalism Triumphs in the West and Fails Everywhere Else (New York: Basic Books, 2000), 20-21.

ENDNOTES

41. Ibid., 20.

42. Winston Churchill. "Speech in the House of Commons" 11 November 1947 in 206-207 The Official Report, House of Commons, vol. 444. 1947.

43. C.S. Lewis, *The Voyage of the Dawn Treader* (New York: HarperCollins, 2008), 59.

44. C.S. Lewis, *Mere Christianity* (New York: HarperOne, 2015) 28-29.

45. C.S. Lewis, "De Descriptione Temporum" (lecture, Cambridge University, Cambridge, 1954).

46. C.S. Lewis, "Is Progress Possible?: Willing Slaves of the Welfare State," in *God in the Dock* (Grand Rapids: Eerdmans, 2014).

Made in the USA
San Bernardino, CA
27 July 2016